Mordecai Richler (1931–   )

KERRY MCSWEENEY

Mordecai Richler (1931–)

KERRY MCSWEENEY

Biography

THE 1931 CENSUS revealed that the total population of the greater Montreal area was just over one million, of whom almost fifty-eight thousand were Jewish. Comparison with the 1921 census showed that within the Montreal area Jews had already begun to move from the inner city wards of Saint Louis and Laurier to the more affluent districts of Westmount and Outremont.[1] This migration accelerated during the next two decades but never included the parents of Mordecai Richler. It was the predominantly Jewish, working-class ghetto — "an all but self-contained world made up of five streets, Clark, St. Urbain, Waverley, Esplanade, and Jeanne Mance, bounded by the Main, on one side, and Park Avenue, on the other"[2] — into which the future novelist was born on 27 January 1931 and in which he grew up.

Richler's forbears had emigrated to Canada from Russia and Poland early in the century. One grandfather was an Hassid and a scholar who translated the Zohar into modern Hebrew and wrote religious tracts and speeches for rabbis.[3] In Montreal he became a peddler. Richler's father was a junk dealer, and his mother, after her divorce in the early 1940s, rented rooms and cooked meals for neighbourhood bachelors.[4] The son attended the Talmud Torah primary school and Baron Byng High School (called Fletcher's Field in his novels). Since his grades were sufficiently mediocre to keep him out of McGill University, it was while attending Sir George Williams College that Richler discovered that he wanted to be a writer.

This discovery ended his formal education. At the age of nineteen, Richler left for Europe, where he remained for two years, living in London, on the Spanish island of Ibiza, and in Paris, where his literary acquaintances included Terry Southern,

Mason Hoffenberg, Mavis Gallant, Alan Temko, and James Baldwin.[5] When Richler returned to Canada in 1952, he worked as a news editor for the CBC and began revising his first novel, *The Acrobats*, for which André Deutsch Ltd., the London publisher, had made an offer (one of their advisers was the distinguished British critic Walter Allen).[6] In 1954 Richler returned to London, where he was to live for the next eighteen years, and where in 1959 he married Florence Wood, from which union four children were born during the 1960s.

The Acrobats came out in 1954; in the next five years, Richler published three more novels: *Son of a Smaller Hero* (1955), *A Choice of Enemies* (1957), and his best-known work, *The Apprenticeship of Duddy Kravitz* (1959). His later novels have been much slower in coming: *The Incomparable Atuk* (*Stick Your Neck Out* is the title of the American edition) appeared in 1963; *Cocksure*, in 1968; *St. Urbain's Horseman*, in 1971; and *Joshua Then and Now*, in 1980. To this list should be appended *The Street* (1969), a medley of stories and memories that nostalgically but unsentimentally recreate the Saint Urbain Street world of Richler's childhood and adolescence.

In addition to his novels, Richler has written frequently (some would say indiscriminately) on cultural subjects for a wide variety of magazines and journals.[7] It is this body of writing that established Richler as an *enfant terrible* of Canadian letters and raised the hackles of literary and cultural nationalists. The best of his reviews and periodical essays were collected in *Hunting Tigers under Glass: Essays and Reports* (1968) and *Shovelling Trouble* (1972). Their contents are rearranged and recycled in *Notes on an Endangered Species and Others* (New York, 1974) and *The Great Comic Book Heroes and Other Essays* (1978). Richler edited *Canadian Writing Today* for Penguin Books in 1970; his excellent children's book *Jacob Two-Two Meets the Hooded Fang* appeared in 1975; and in 1977 he supplied a text for *Images of Spain*, a collection of photographs by Peter Christopher. Richler has also written film scripts: his credits include *No Love for Johnnie* (1961), *Life at the Top* (1965), and *The Apprenticeship of Duddy Kravitz* (1974), the last two of which were directed by Richler's close friend Ted Kotcheff.[8]

In 1972 Richler returned to live in Montreal and settled his family in Westmount, premier emblem of the Canadian WASP establishment and the epitome of the social goals of many of his Saint Urbain Street contemporaries. Now in his fifties, Richler would seem to have attained most of his own worldly goals: he is one of Canada's better-known contemporary writers, and one of the more distinguished. His honours and awards include a Guggenheim fellowship in creative writing, a Canada Council senior arts fellowship, the 1968 Governor General's Award for fiction and essays (*Cocksure* and *Hunting Tigers under Glass*), and the 1971 Governor General's Award for fiction (*St. Urbain's Horseman*). *Jacob Two-Two* won two awards, as did the film version of *Duddy Kravitz*. Richler has also been writer-in-residence at Sir George Williams University and Carleton University. But his appointment in 1976 to the editorial board of the Book-of-the-Month Club was a reminder that for a serious writer Richler has maintained a high profile and that over the years he has cultivated his talents as an entertainer as well as his skills as a novelist. It is as much the former as the latter that has won Mordecai Richler a wide audience, not only in Canada but in the United States and Britain as well.

Tradition and Milieu

Mordecai Richler is not only one of Canada's better-known novelists; he is also the best-known critic of the literary and cultural nationalism that began to flourish in Canada in the late 1960s. Richler's critique of what he regards as the provincial and regressive tendencies of many of his younger creative contemporaries and of the "embarrassingly boosterish"[9] quality of much of the writing about Canadian literature is rooted in his conception of the literary tradition and milieu to which he belongs. As Robert Fulford has remarked, "...we have to remember Richler's beginnings as a writer in a Canadian literary culture very different from the one we know now. As Richler saw it a quarter of a century ago — so his essays would suggest — Canadian literature was dominated by gentlemen amateurs who believed more in 'Canadian' than in 'literature.' Richler's generation, or some part of it, saw it as their task to reverse this tendency, and to reach beyond Canada towards the literary standards of Britain and the United States."[10]

Richler himself put it this way in "The Elected Squares," a series of articles on Canada which he wrote in 1961 for a British journal:

> We were, as I recall it, embarrassed to be Canadians. Charged with it, we always had a self-deprecating joke ready.
>
> At college, during the late Forties, when we began to read the *New Republic* and the *New Statesman and Nation*, and one or perhaps two of us dared to say out loud in a tavern, "I'm going to be a writer," the immediate rejoinder was, "What? You're going to be a *Canadian* writer. Hey, *he's* going to be a Canadian writer."
>
> We actually had a course on Canadian writing at our college. The mimeographed text listed the author, dimensions, number of pages and photographs, if any, of nearly every book that had ever been published here. There were, at the time, several Canadian "little magazines" but we would have considered it a stigma to have our stories printed in any one of them, just as the most damaging criticism you could make of another man's poetry was, "Ryerson is publishing it in Toronto."
>
> London and New York were the places we looked to for all our excitements. We had never had, in the literary history of our own country, a magazine that young people might have responded to, like *Penguin New Writing*, and what really bound us together in those days was a shared sense of how comic our country was. We appeared to be surrounded by the ridiculous.[11]

This did not mean that Canadian values inevitably led to inferior or parochial writing; Richler did point out that "...self-conscious Canadianism has made for at least two writers who deserve attention, Hugh MacLennan and Robertson Davies."[12] And five years before, he had spoken of the short fiction of Morley Callaghan as "the best stories or prose I have read by an English-Canadian writer who is truly Canadian" (Cohen, p. 28). At the same time, Richler — a Jew from the Montreal ghetto — did observe that MacLennan and Davies were both "literary gents," whose popularity in the United States he thought owing to "nostalgia for the unhurried nineteenth century."[13] And further evidence of Richler's estrangement from the gentility of the native literary strain is seen in his 1956 pronouncement that "...the two best novels that have been written in Canada are by Canadians in quotes...": Malcolm Lowry's *Under the Volcano* and Brian Moore's *Judith Hearne* (Cohen, p. 28).

It was America, not Canada, that provided the young Mordecai Richler with a usable literary tradition and a dynamic modernist milieu: "...I consider myself an American," he remarked in 1956, "and the first modern novels I read were American. I read Dos Passos and Hemingway and Fitzgerald and Faulkner, and these are people who influenced me a great deal. And of course my attitudes are American, and even coming here [he is speaking as an expatriate living in Europe] is a North American convention..." (Cohen, p. 34). This explains why Richler's first novel, *The Acrobats*, is full of the techniques, mannerisms, and attitudes of modern American writers—so full that a reviewer could rightly speak of its uniqueness as "intelligent, contemporary *pastiche*."[14] There are the newsreel collages à la Dos Passos, the nightmare paragraphs out of Henry Miller, and the startling interpolation of a direct address to the Rio Turia, in which the debased, sordid present and romantic, chivalric past are juxtaposed in a manner all too reminiscent of the presentation of the Thames in T. S. Eliot's *The Waste Land*.

More than any other precursor it is Hemingway who dominates *The Acrobats*. The characters and the setting — English-speaking expatriates and visitors in a Spanish city at fiesta time— are those of the last half of *The Sun Also Rises*. When André Bennett, the central character, converses with his beloved Toni, the used but essentially innocent Spanish girl, a fisherman's daughter from Ibiza, we are back with Robert Jordan and Maria in *For Whom the Bell Tolls:* "In the summer they would take us out in the boats and we would jump overboard and swim. The water was very cool, and there was always the taste of salt in our mouths."[15] (It was, however, not until Richler's second novel that the central character asks his beloved if the earth moved during their lovemaking.) When André thinks that *love* "is one of the words that is no longer any good. Like *courage, soul, beautiful, honour,* and so many others" (p. 48), we know that he has read Chapter xxvii of *A Farewell to Arms*. And when an-

5

other character reflects that "...those days at the front constituted the only moment of truth he had known..." (p. 133), we remember "Soldier's Home" from *In Our Time* as well as the mystique of the bullfight celebrated in *Death in the Afternoon*. As these last two quotations from *The Acrobats* suggest, the influences on Richler of his American seniors were not simply those of style and manner; they also included a self-consciously serious existential stance and a taste for big questions. In 1956 Richler spoke (in Hemingwayesque cadences) of what was to become a central concern of his fiction: the baffled liberal humanist's search for "values with which in this time a man can live with honour" (Cohen, p. 38). (By honour Richler seemed to mean something like the Spanish concept of *pundonor* as it is expounded in Chapter ix of *Death in the Afternoon*.) In all three of the early novels there is an oppressive *Weltschmerz*: "...is there any hope?" (p. 204) is the question asked on the last page of *The Acrobats*; "If God did not exist, everything would be lawful" is the Dostoevskian epigraph to *Son of a Smaller Hero*; and, like its predecessors, *A Choice of Enemies* shows a lost generation no longer able to fortify itself by fighting fascism in the Spanish civil war or World War II and increasingly demoralized by the psychological aftermath of the Holocaust and the postwar paralysis of the political and moral will.

In his early novels, these serious concerns were so insistently presented and heavily underscored as to suggest on the part of the outsetting novelist from Canada a deliberate attempt to graft himself onto the main trunk of modernist anxiety. Beginning with his fourth novel, *The Apprenticeship of Duddy Kravitz*, these same concerns begin to find expression through the different artistic modes of comedy, wicked satire, and black comedy. This significant change in key is related to two other important influences on Richler's fiction. One of them (to which more attention needs to be paid by his commentators) is the literary form of the screenplay or film script. Through working in this medium, Richler learned to set a faster narrative pace, to use quick cuts and jump cuts, and to add flavour, zest, and entertaining set pieces to his fiction. He also experimented with including a film script within the text of his novels, a device used with superb comic effect in *Duddy Kravitz* (the Marxist barmitzvah documentary) and also deployed in *Cocksure* and *St.*

Urbain's Horseman. But it is important to note that despite these influences Richler remains at best dubious about film, which he seems to regard more as a danger to humane values than as a serious medium of artistic expression. Consider, for example, what the movies have done to Polly Morgan ("creature of a generation") in *Cocksure*: "...living with her was...a mixed pleasure. If, for instance, she looked up a complicated meal in *Larousse*, he had to reconcile himself to a hasty sandwich secretly consumed in the toilet, for she was bound to cut from pondering the sauce to serving coffee and brandy, just as she dissolved from his cupping a breast to the gratifying pillow talk that followed the most satisfying lovemaking."[16]

The second late-germinating influence on Richler is that of black humourists like Terry Southern and Mason Hoffenberg, his Paris acquaintances of the early 1950s. But Richler also traces his black-humour side back to Nathanael West, Waugh, and Céline and agrees that *Cocksure*, which among his novels has the highest concentration of black humour, belongs to the same genre as do *Miss Lonelyhearts*, *The Day of the Locust*, *The Magic Christian*, and *Candy*. Richler traced these connections in a 1974 interview with John Metcalf, during which he made two shrewd comments on the genre: that an expatriate writer might be drawn to the presentational techniques of black humour as a way of disguising increasing gaps in firsthand knowledge of "his natural material"; and that "the biggest sacrifice" the black humourist makes is the forfeiture of the reader's sympathy since "there's *nobody* to sympathize with...."[17]

Such are the main currents of literary influence that run together in the fiction of Mordecai Richler. Yet if an overview of his literary traditions and milieu stopped here, a false impression would be created of the nature of Richler's fiction and of what — since Saint Urbain Street is within its borders — can only be regarded as its essentially Canadian ambiance. As we shall see, one of the most pervasive givens of Richler's fiction — as subject matter, theme, moral precipitate, and atmospheric tincture — is Jewishness. It is, so to speak, not the tradition and milieu which Richler chose, but the tradition and milieu which chose him. The Saint Urbain Street of his youth remains for Richler the ground of his identity and distinctiveness as a novelist. Again and again in his fiction, he has returned, Antaeus-like, to this soil for strength, and it is here, if anywhere, that the distinctively Canadian nature of his imagination is to be found. George Woodcock has even argued that "what his novels suggest is that 'the idea of a Jew' is very much like the idea of a Canadian, for Canada is a land of minorities, regions, disguised ghettoes. In that lies Richler's appeal to his countrymen, and the reason why...he is never considered as other than a Canadian writer."[18]

Critical Overview and Context

The first criticism any contemporary writer receives comes in reviews, and during the 1950s it was mainly in that form that criticism of Richler appeared. Despite their glaring technical and stylistic weaknesses, the first three novels did not fare badly when they were placed in the hands of competent reviewers. The *Spectator*, *The New York Times Book Review*, and the *Saturday Review* all had positive things to say about *The Acrobats*, and *The Times Literary Supplement* [London] accentuated the positive in its reviews of *Son of a Smaller Hero* ("there can be no doubt of his prodigal talent") and *A Choice of Enemies* ("a thoughtful and lively novel") (Darling, pp. 193–95). On the home front, Claude Bissell, in the 1954 "Letters in Canada" roundup in the *University of Toronto Quarterly*, described *The Acrobats* as "heavy with undisciplined emotion" but also noted its "pleasant mastery of colloquial dialogue, and...skill in handling the typical modern techniques of discontinuity."[19] A year later, in the same forum, Bissell welcomed *Son of a Smaller Hero* as "certainly one of the best portraits that we have ever had in our literature of a particular Canadian group and place."[20] And, in *Queen's Quarterly*, Robert Weaver noted that the same novel was written "with real emotional and intellectual force" and rightly predicted that Richler was going to be "a tough, prolific and vigorous professional, who will be quite capable of writing poor things, but who ought to have a number of serious and exciting novels in him."[21]

The Apprenticeship of Duddy Kravitz was widely and on the whole positively reviewed, though some were given pause by the rawness of the subject matter and the dark (shading at times into black) comic energy. In *The New York Times Book Review*,

Florence Crowther called the novel "unnecessarily vulgar"; in *The Montrealer*, Constance Beresford-Howe pronounced its style uncouth and its comedy "threadbare"; and, in *The Dalhousie Review*, D.J. Dooley found the novel's theme trite and its title character "utterly without decency" (Darling, pp.195–96). From the point of view of the 1980s, the genteel standards of these reviewers, which recall Somerset Maugham's revulsed animadversions of 1954 on the central character of Kingsley Amis' *Lucky Jim*, seem quaint, if not antedeluvian. But they are an epitome of the negative criticism that Richler's novels have received from belletristic and moralistic commentators, and a useful reminder of the middlebrow literary mores of the 1950s with which the young Richler had to contend. Another reminder is Nathan Cohen's intemperate 1958 attack, "Heroes of the Richler View," which was one of the first critical articles devoted to Richler's work. This preposterous philippic by an established lightweight of the Canadian cultural scene condemned most of Richler's characters as not worth caring about and blasted his first two novels for "the slovenly, undisciplined craftsmanship, the unsettling ambivalence of thought, the contrived violence and abundant bedwetting."[22]

After *Duddy Kravitz*, Richler could be reckoned to have a fictional canon, and during the 1960s several overviews of his work appeared. Two critics levelled a charge that, *mutatis mutandis*, was to be reiterated in the following years as the winds of literary nationalism began to rise in Canada. In 1964 Naïm Kattan argued that the influence of American pop culture had prevented Richler from achieving his true potential,[23] and in 1966 Warren Tallman, noting the slowdown in his fictional output, wondered whether Richler had lost touch with his main sources of inspiration: his childhood environment and idealistic politics.[24]

Reviews of the 1963 entertainment, *The Incomparable Atuk*, were numerous, accurate, and favourable; those of the 1968 black comedy *Cocksure* were also favourable, but rather more interesting because the novel was more controversial. In Britain, Richler received a negative notice from W.H. Smith, the country's major bookstore chain, which refused to stock the novel; John Wain and Philip Toynbee both praised its satire but raised questions about the author's moral stance; and

Anthony Burgess distinguished between the book and the world it depicts and argued that only the latter was obscene (Darling, pp. 198–99). In America, Leslie Fiedler also admired the novel but regretted that it was insufficiently obscene.[25]

In 1971 *St. Urbain's Horseman* was enthusiastically welcomed by most Canadian reviewers and critics. It was rightly identified as the big novel that had been expected from Richler for almost a decade and praised as a cumulative work containing a synthesis of the subjects, themes, and concerns of his earlier novels. In short, it was hailed as a major work. Outside Canada, however, *St. Urbain's Horseman* was more critically assessed. Much as he wanted to admire the novel, Roger Sale in *The New York Review of Books* was forced to conclude that it was "a raconteur's story, shaggy and timed, incapable of testing anything";[26] and the *The Times Literary Supplement* reviewer found the novel "occasionally funny, observant and apposite, but more often only crudely and woodenly facetious"; serious concerns were "swamped by accumulations of the Jewish detail which Mr. Richler senses so well and retails so unfailingly, submerged in a flood of joking which misses few opportunities yet hits surprisingly few targets."[27]

The year 1971 also saw the publication of two books about Mordecai Richler, each of which belonged to a recently established series devoted to the work of Canadian writers. Even though published too soon to include consideration of *St. Urbain's Horseman*, both books gave witness to the fact that Richler had become a major Canadian novelist. G. David Sheps's *Mordecai Richler*, in the Critical Views on Canadian Writers series, was a collection of previously published critical pieces, including a number of those cited above. George Woodcock's *Mordecai Richler*, a sixty-four-page critical study by Canada's leading man of letters, offered an excellent introduction to Richler's fiction. (It should be supplemented by Woodcock's long and insightful review of *St. Urbain's Horseman*.)[28]

With the rapid growth during the 1970s in the study of Canadian literature in universities, it was inevitable that Richler's novels would become the subject of academic literary criticism and that individual texts would be given detailed scrutiny. Articles began to appear with weighty titles like "Of Self, Temporal Cubism, and Metaphor: Mordecai Richler's *St. Urbain's Horse-*

man"[29] and "The Golem as Metaphor for Art: The Monster Takes Meaning in *St. Urbain's Horseman.*"[30] (An excellent early analysis of a single text was George Bowering's "And the Sun Goes Down: Richler's First Novel" [1966];[31] of other perceptive analyses, I shall mention only Bruce Stovel's introduction to the New Canadian Library edition of *A Choice of Enemies.*)[32] Some of these studies concentrated attention on the Jewish themes and resonances of Richler's novels and thereby served as a salutary corrective to the para-critical attacks on Richler's depiction of Jewish characters which have been made over the years by superficial or noncompetent readers. Other academic critics tended to make Richler's novels into grist for the thematic mill: discussions of his work began to appear in studies with titles like *Patterns of Isolation in English-Canadian Fiction,*[33] *The Haunted Wilderness: The Gothic and Grotesque in Canadian Fiction,*[34] and *Sex and Violence in the Canadian Novel: The Ancestral Present.*[35]

A full listing of critical studies of Richler — including theses, dissertations, and selected book reviews — is found in Michael Darling's "Mordecai Richler: An Annotated Bibliography."[36] Darling also lists the four important interviews with Richler (by Nathan Cohen, Donald Cameron, Graeme Gibson, and John Metcalf).

Richler's Works

Over the years, in articles and interviews, Richler has talked about his informing concerns as a writer of serious fiction. One of them is what may be called the-way-it-was impulse: no matter where he makes his home, Richler feels "forever rooted in Montreal's St. Urbain Street. That was my time, my place, and I have elected myself to get it right."[37] The author's note to his second novel states that although the characters and their situations are fictional, "...all the streets described in this book are real streets, and the seasons, tempers and moods are those of Montreal as I remember them...."[38] The particulars are remembered with freshness and vividness, and retain their affective power, because they were first experienced with the special perceptual intensities of childhood. For Richler, as for the poet

A. M. Klein, another product of the Montreal "ghetto streets,"
the seasons, tempers, and mood of childhood and early youth are

> Dear to me always with the virgin joy
> Of the first flowering of senses five.
> . . . .
> . . . Never was I more alive.
> All days thereafter are a dying off,
> A wandering away
> From home and the familiar. . . .
> . . . .
> No other day is ever like that day.[39]

Saint Urbain Street did not just confer on Richler an indelible
sense of identity. To use George Eliot's phrase, his "present past"
is also his "root of piety"[40] and the ground of those humane
concerns in his fiction to which Richler has more than once called
attention. He has spoken of the writer "as a kind of loser's
advocate"[41] and in 1971 insisted that running through his novels,
but grasped by "almost nobody," was "a persistent attempt to
make a case for the ostensibly unsympathetic man."[42] It is not
surprising that this was grasped by few readers, for wicked
satire, black humour, and what I shall presently call deconstructive energy would not seem the natural channels for the
expression of humane concern. In the stories and reminiscences
of *The Street*, however, where memory and a street-wise piety
flow freely, one finds passages in which the still, sad music of
ordinary humanity is heard. Here, for example, is the finest paragraph in the book (the year is 1968 and Richler is describing the
older Jews who are reluctant to move from the ghetto):

> . . . many of the grandparents still cling to the Main. Their
> children cannot in many cases persuade them to leave. So
> you still see them there, drained and used up by the
> struggle. They sit on kitchen chairs next to the coke freezer
> in the cigar store, dozing with a fly swatter held in a mottled
> hand. You find them rolling their own cigarettes and
> studying the obituary columns in the *Star* on the steps
> outside the Jewish Library. The women still peel potatoes
> under the shade of a winding outside staircase. Old men

still watch the comings and goings from the balcony above, a blanket spread over their legs and a little bag of polly seeds on their lap. As in the old days the sinking house with the crooked floor is right over the store or the wholesaler's, or maybe next door to the scrap yard. Only today the store and the junk yard are shut down. Signs for Sweet Caporal cigarettes or old election posters have been nailed in over the missing windows. There are spider webs everywhere.[43]

A third major concern of Richler's fiction is satiric; its direction is pointed up in his comment that he is especially interested in criticizing "the things I believe in or I'm attached to" — liberal values, Jews, Canada (Cameron, p. 117). But what Richler has most consistently emphasized about his work is its moral basis. For him the novelist's task is "fundamentally a moral one"; unlike the commercial writer, the serious writer works "within a moral tradition" (Gibson, p. 271). As early as the 1956 interview with Nathan Cohen, Richler spoke of his compulsion "to say what I feel about values and about people living in a time when to my mind there is no agreement on values" (Cohen, p. 29). In 1971 he again emphasized that "from the very beginning, in a faltering way," he had been "most engaged... with values, and with honour. I would say I'm a moralist, really" (Cameron, p. 124).

The extent to which Richler has realized these dominant concerns and the degree to which he has been able to harmonize them and make them complement each other are appropriate gauges for a critical assessment of his eight novels. One must first add, however, that there is another important determinant of Richler's fiction, of which the author himself, as well as his commentators (except for Graeme Gibson in certain penetrating pages of his interview with Richler), seem largely unaware, and which certainly does work at cross purposes with the other concerns of his fiction. I speak of a certain deconstructive energy which at times tends to undermine Richler's constructive concerns as a satirist and moralist, a demoralizing force which it is hard not to regard as being rooted in a dark negating vision, an inhumane vision, of human existence. Sometimes this force makes for discontinuities in the novels, like the unresolved contrast between the "scene of soft tender bliss," "a beautifully subdued fade-out," with which *Joshua Then and Now* concludes and "the spiteful bile that's accumulated like sediment for more than 400 pages."⁴⁴ At other times, when this force is present only weakly or recessively, it tends to manifest itself in episodes and emphases that seem tasteless and gratuitous, like Virgil's magazine for health handicappers in *Duddy Kravitz*; or the pedophiliac pedagogy of Miss Ryerson in *Cocksure*, who combines traditional educational principles with a newfound taste for fellatio; or the late-blooming grossness of Esther Shapiro, mother of the central character of *Joshua Then and Now*, who during a pro-abortion demonstration on Parliament Hill waits until the television cameras are turned on her before brandishing a placard which reads "Smelly it may be / But my cunt belongs to me," and who as Esty Blossom performs in a porno film: there she was, her son reflects, "up there on the big screen blowing men half her age."⁴⁵ Some commentators have rightly noted how these and other vignettes have weakened the satiric, humane, and moral concerns of Richler's fiction. But what has not been sufficiently noticed is that when Richler's deconstructive energy, however subversive of his constructive intentions as a novelist, is strongly present, the result is the most imaginatively exciting and compelling passages in his fiction.

It is this energy, together with his concern with values and his sense of Jewishness, that makes Richler's first novel, *The Acrobats*, something more than what over a quarter of a century later he described as "just a very young man's novel. Hopelessly derivative....I wasn't writing in my own voice at all. I was imitating people."⁴⁶ The setting is Valencia in the early 1950s during the city's annual fiesta. A sense of place is conveyed through an impasto of portentous and sordid detail: the processional *fallas*, each one "posturing like a predatory ogre in the darkness" (p. 50), all but one of which are burned and exploded at the climax of the fiesta; heat smelling of "rancid food, children with soiled underwear, uncovered garbage, venereal diseases, sweat and boils, pimpled adolescents with one leg and a stump for another" (p. 135); tourists who "felt the gas and acids contained in their bellies. And in their mouths were yellow teeth and stuck bits of meat..." (p. 127); and human detritus — a crippled beggar, an old man picking up cigarette butts from the gutter, prostitutes, vagrants huddled at night around a twig fire underneath a bridge.

Against this demoralizing background are placed a number of foreign characters, each representing a part of the equally demoralizing spectrum of contemporary values. There are Barney Larkin, the affluent Jewish American businessman, vulgar in manner and banal in thought, and his gentile wife, Jessie, who "wandered through life not experiencing things but accumulating memories" (p. 85) and whom another character perceives as generically American: "No dental odours, armpits shaven, no facial hairs, birthmarks removed in early childhood. No possibilities of human smells" (p. 90). There is Derek Raymond, once a serious writer who experienced ennobling moments of truth fighting for the Republic in the Spanish civil war, now an alcoholic, a homosexual, and a convert to Roman Catholicism; there is Chaim, whose "profoundly expressive" eyes are those "of a melancholy clown, the eyes of a man who had absorbed so much of anguish that he was inclined to defend his human vulnerability behind a deprecating jest" (p. 19); there is the patrician German who hangs herself with the old skipping rope her brother had once used in training for the Olympics, signing her suicide note "Theresa Kraus Ph.D." (p. 192); and there is her evil brother, Roger Kraus, an ex-officer in the German army, an anti-Semite, and a sadist, whose murder of André Bennett on the last night of the fiesta is the climax of *The Acrobats*.

A fledgling painter from Montreal, at twenty-three the coeval of his creator, André is the central character in *The Acrobats* and the most valueless. He is also the first in a series of Richler protagonists — baffled seekers after meaning who either have never known, or find slipping from their grasp, the conviction and the singlemindedness that are the prerequisites of right living and efficacious action. André belongs to a "new post-war generation" afflicted with spiritual and political acedia and "waiting, waiting for something they were at a loss to explain" (p. 33). He knows "all the things that he is against but he still doesn't know what he is for" (p. 36) and cannot even believe "in the validity of... [his] own anger" (p. 59); he has no Lincoln Brigade to join and unlike his friend Guillermo, the *engagé* communist revolutionary, does not know how to act and guesses that his crime "is that I haven't chosen" (p. 72). As he lies dying, André's last thought is: "*All I ask is that I know what's going on. That's all. Never mind the cigarette. Just knowing...*" (p. 176).

The ostensible reason why Kraus despises and kills André is jealousy: they are both in love with the young prostitute Toni. The deeper reason, which Richler quite lacks the skills to convey effectively, is that there is a deep attraction / repulsion between the two men. Had this been more successfully conveyed, it would have brought into much sharper focus the underlying Jewishness of the novel's vision. For, while the young painter killed by the anti-Semitic German is a gentile from Westmount, the determining event in his past life (and the psychological — as opposed to the ideological or historical — cause of his *Weltschmerz*) had been his love for Ida, the Jewish girl from "a foul-smelling St Dominic Street flat in the heart of the Montreal ghetto" (p. 124), who had died of a botched abortion and whose father on learning of her death had bitterly asked André: "Will you always murder us for your enjoyment?" (p. 124).

André's special affinity with Jewishness gives resonance both to his victim-victimizer symbiosis with Kraus and to the reflections of Chaim, who is in other respects a rather superficial characterization — a wise Jew from central casting. The British critic A. Alvarez has observed that "if there is any religious tone at all in the modern arts, it is a certain Jewishness. I mean Judaism not as a narrow orthodoxy but as a force working perennially on the side of sanity. . . . it is empirical in its attitude to experience, pragmatic and hard-minded. Since these seem to be the qualities most valued and demanded now the writer becomes, almost of necessity, either a real or, in John Berryman's words, an 'imaginary' Jew. He is concerned, that is, not with beliefs but with sceptical, non-idealistic survival.'"[47] This "certain Jewishness" finds expression in Chaim's reflections: that ". . . there is no idea or cause that will save us all. Salvation is personal" (p. 116); that *Nothing is ever resolved, but it's always worth it*" (p. 202); and that, in the last words of the novel, "There is always hope. Always. There has to be" (p. 204). But these are virtually the only inspiriting notes sounded in *The Acrobats*, the only rays of light piercing the darkness of the young novelist's vision.

Jewish Montreal, touched on only in passing in Richler's first novel, is both the setting and the generic subject of his second. In *Son of a Smaller Hero*, the streets and inhabitants of the ghetto are pungently described, as is the street in Outremont frequented by the well-to-do Jews who have made it out of the ghetto

MORDECAI RICHLER

("Buick convertibles and Cadillacs parked on both sides: a street without a past" [p. 17]). Also described are the Jewish resort towns north of Montreal, which reflect the generational and class differences of the city: on the one hand, demotic Shawbridge, its beach "a field of spiky grass and tree stumps" where "plump, middle-aged women, their flesh burned pink, spread out blankets and squatted in their bras and bloomers, playing poker, smoking and drinking cokes" while their husbands "set up cardtables and chairs and played pinochle solemnly, smoking foul cigars and cursing the sun" (p. 57); on the other hand, Sainte-Agathe-des-Monts, with its arriviste and acculturated Jews, its riding academy and summer camps "sometimes with a child-psychiatrist in attendance" (p. 194).

The Adler family is the novel's specific subject, its microcosm of Montreal Jewry. Through the family, Richler presents one aspect of his novel's central theme: that the ghetto is a psychological as well as a physical place. It "has no real walls and no true dimensions. The walls are the habit of atavism and the dimensions are an illusion. But the ghetto exists all the same" (p. 14). The Adlers "lived in a cage and that cage, with all its faults, had justice and safety and a kind of felicity. . . . As much as they might condemn one another in their own homes they presented a solid front to the Goyim" (pp. 39–40). The family head is the patriarchal Melech, whose rigid dignity and inflexible will personify the ghetto values of first-generation Jews. Several of his ten children are representative of other parts of the Montreal Jewish spectrum. Particularly important are two of the brothers: Wolf, Melech's firstborn, a loser who "could not understand why he had such awful luck" (p. 126) and who is entirely defined by his dependent relationship with his father and by the values of Panofsky's Cigar and Soda; and Max, who has made it to Outremont and Sainte-Agathe. Affluent and vulgar (he recalls Barney Larkin in The Acrobats), Max represents a debasement of ghetto dignity and of Jewishness: he uses anti-Semitism to rationalize his dubious business practices, reflects at his brother's funeral that he puts his trust, not in the God of his fathers, but in Dow Jones, and is having it off with his secretary, a blonde gentile who despises him.

The world of Son of a Smaller Hero is rendered with the same crude vigour, borrowed styles, and technical gaucherie as is the setting of *The Acrobats* (not for nothing have the pair been referred to as Richler's two first novels).[48] Particularly infelicitous in the second novel are the interior monologues assigned to a number of characters during the funeral service for Wolf. They are the first instance in Richler's fiction of the satiric caricature he will later employ so effectively; but the monologues are overdone in their own right and seriously out of key with the density of realistic detail and seriousness of the rest of the novel. This density — Richler's quantitative success, so to speak, in getting down on paper the way it was in his time and place—is one of the reasons why, for all its faults of construction and technique, *Son of a Smaller Hero* is an interesting and engaging novel. The other reason is the more important: the novel's passionate apprehension of a serious theme and the energetic sincerity of Richler's attempt to articulate the theme through the literary form best adapted to the study of cultural aspiration and of the pressures exerted on an individual by family and society.

The principal character and thematic centre of *Son of a Smaller Hero* is Noah Adler, the only son of Wolf and the oldest grandson of Melech, who had hoped that the boy would grow up to be the light of his declining years. In some respects, Noah resembles André Bennett: both are young, high-minded, and confused; like his predecessor, Noah realizes "it is necessary to say yes to something" (p. 31) and is similarly caught between two worlds — one dead, to use Matthew Arnold's phrase, the other powerless to be born. Noah is, however, a more interesting character and more rounded characterization because the world that seems dead to him is not an intellectual abstraction but the palpable world of the Jewish ghetto. At one point, Noah reflects that "*I should have had the right to begin with my birth*" (p. 62). But such permission is given to no man, and though he has turned his back on the world of Melech Adler, he still feels its pull ("Seen from a distance, it seemed full of tender possibilities, anachronistic but beautiful" [p. 31]) and is later to realize that despite his exertions, "I'm not free yet" (p. 84). Noah's quandary has none of *The Waste Land* chic of André's; it is rather a freshly realized, Canadian version of a story enacted over and over again in the prose fiction of the nineteenth and twentieth centuries: of how, in the words of *The Mill on the Floss*, the "oppressive narrowness" of a home environment acted on young natures "that in the onward tendency of human things have risen above the mental level of the generation before them, to which they have been nevertheless tied by the strongest fibres of their hearts."⁴⁹

Noah's struggle between two worlds is focused by the opposing pulls of the two women in his life. One of them is his mother, Leah, whose unhappy marriage has led her to cling all the more strongly to her only child and who, after she is widowed, quickly develops some of the less attractive traits proverbially associated with Jewish mothers. The other is Noah's gentile mistress, Miriam, "the first modern, sophisticated woman whom he had ever met" (p. 49). Miriam is one of the most interesting and rounded characterizations in the novel. She is given an unhappy childhood on Queen Street in Griffintown near the Montreal waterfront and a failing marriage to Theo (Noah's English professor at college); and since the point of view from which their affair is dramatized is not restricted to Noah, the reader gains a sympathetic sense of Miriam's vulnerability and anxiety. At the end of the novel, after she has returned to her husband, Richler even provides a sharply observed New Year's Eve party scene involving Miriam, Theo, and their tiresomely bright crowd ("That's phallic," one observes after a balloon is popped with a cigarette [p. 220]) in which one is shown that Miriam has begun to go to pieces.

Considerable space is devoted to the Noah-Miriam relationship, and George Woodcock is right to say that their affair is "less intrinsically important than the space it takes up in the novel might at first sight lead one to assume."⁵⁰ In the context of Richler's canon, however, the affair is extremely interesting because for virtually the only time in his fiction the author attempted an in-depth, rounded characterization of a female character, the one exception to his own generalizations: ". . . I've never written very well about women. I think my feminine characters tend to be one-dimensional. . . . the women in my novels tend to be rather idealized creatures, and not written about with the greatest confidence, I'm afraid" (Gibson, pp. 287, 288).

But it is Noah's relationship to his Jewishness that is the dominant thread in Son of a Smaller Hero. Just beyond the middle of the novel, by which point fissures have begun to appear in their affair (for one thing, "the petty anxieties and the duties" of his relationship with Miriam were "beginning to duplicate his relationship with his mother" [p. 140]), the death of Wolf Adler forces Noah back into the world of the ghetto. Wolf had died trying to save from a fire a locked box that was his father's, Melech's, secret possession. The search for his body among the burnt ruins of the family junkyard is described in detail; another chapter describes Wolf's funeral service; and a third, the custom of *shivah* — the seven days of family mourning in the house of the departed.

It is during this time, through learning the contents of Melech's box and sensing its symbolic ramifications, that Noah comes to as much understanding as the novel offers of his inheritance as an Adler and as a Jew. Wolf had tried to save the box because he thought it contained money to which he felt he had a right. But what could money have done to remedy the poverty of imagination and character — the ghetto void — epitomized in the contents of the pathetic diary found by Noah in Wolf's secret box, the false-bottomed lower drawer of his desk? What Melech's box contained was a stack of old love letters written in Russian and Polish and photographs of a plump blonde girl: for Melech too had once yearned for escape from the walls of the ghetto, a freedom symbolized, as for Noah and even the awful Max, by the love of a gentile.

The symbolic suggestiveness of locked boxes, secret lives, and supra-ghetto shiksas is anything but conceptually cleancut; the symbols intensify rather than clarify, and one might observe that in his second novel, which is explicitly about Jewishness, Richler seems more ambivalent about its positive value than he and his spokesman Chaim were in *The Acrobats*, a novel almost entirely peopled by gentiles. But the closing pages of *Son of a Smaller Hero* do at least bring Noah's process of growth into sharper focus. Following his decision to leave Montreal for Europe, Leah dies of a heart attack, and Melech, though he remains unyielding, feels sorrow and self-rebuke. At their final meeting, Noah sums up for his grandfather what more than anything else he has learned during the novel: "I can no more leave you, my mother, or my father's memory, that I can renounce myself. But I can refuse to take part in this..." (p. 230). This is not a great clarification, and Noah's inability to finish his last sentence suggests that he has a good deal more to learn about life. But what he has come to realize is a necessary first step over the threshold into adult life, and it is at this threshold that *Bildungsromane* like *Son of a Smaller Hero* usually end. Richler once observed that his novels "break down into two categories readily. There are the naturalistic novels and the straight satires. . . . I guess my ultimate interest is in the novel of character really" (Metcalf, p. 73). This terminology is unfortunate: "novel of character," though not inaccurate, is too vague to be helpful, and the other two designations are misleading. The former term is presumably meant to cover novels like *Son of a Smaller Hero* and *A Choice of Enemies*, which are realistic in setting and technique, and in which a central figure comes into conflict with himself and with aspects of his society in ways whereby character and values are explored. By the latter term, Richler doubtless meant to designate *The Incomparable Atuk* and *Cocksure*, the two novels he published during the 1960s. Formally speaking, neither is a satire, though both contain satiric elements. *Cocksure* is more black comedy than satire, while *Atuk*, "a much gentler book," "more of a spoof" (Metcalf, p. 74), is a satirical entertainment that collapses into farce.

The subject of *The Incomparable Atuk* is Toronto-based, English-Canadian culture. Its point of view is adumbrated in the novel's epigraph, an observation by Richard H. Rovere that Richler had quoted two years before in his *Spectator* series on "The Elected Squares" (in some ways a précis of the novel): "What would happen in Canada if full sovereignty were invoked and the southern border were sealed tight against American mass culture — if the air-waves were jammed, if all our comic books were embargoed, if only the purest and most uplifting of American cultural commodities were allowed entry? Native industries would take over, obviously. Cut off from American junk, Canada would have to produce her own."[51]

Atuk contains a number of sharply observed and entertainingly exaggerated sketches of producers and exemplars of Canadian cultural schlock: Professor Norman Gore, the modishly anti-American, tenured nationalist; Seymour Bone, whose preposterous philippics — Richler had not forgotten Nathan Cohen's 1958 attack — make him "a sort of reverse Liberace" (p. 75); Harry Snipes the poet, "the most notorious of Canada's middle-aged angries" (p. 59), whose ritual denunciations of his mealy-mouthed countrymen's pallid conventionality does not keep him from accepting the editorship of a kitsch magazine, for which he pseudonymously writes articles with titles like "Why Women from Halifax to Vancouver Menstruate Monthly" and "I Married an Intellectual Cockroach in Calgary"; Dr. Burt Parks, the physical culturalist, who speaks for many of the novel's cultural dunces when he proudly observes, "I'm world-famous, all over Canada" (p. 40); Bette Dolan, Canada's darling, TV star, beauty queen, and foremost swimmer, who, until the moxie Atuk cons her into bed, remains virgin — "Because I belong to the nation. Like Jasper Park or Niagara Falls" (p. 31); and Buck Twentyman, the entrepreneur who wins a major television franchise by promising fifty percent Canadian cultural content, most of it to be aired between five and eight in the morning. There are, in addition, other characters who make cameo appearances, like the trendy Rabbi Seigal and Father Forget, "French Canada's leading philosopher and aesthete" — "'Life,' he said, speaking in English, 'she is happy and life she is sad. Art is the music of the soul'" (p. 136).

The main character in the novel, the string on which the beads of satiric portraiture and comic incident are strung, is the Eskimo Atuk, the success of whose poems, first published for public relations reasons by the Twentyman Fur Co., has brought him from Baffin Bay to Toronto. The big city does not so much corrupt Atuk as provide him with opportunities for corruption, for he is less a naïf than an operator, the noble savage as Sammy Glick. In Toronto he continues to write poems, from the *Howl*-like chant beginning "I have seen the best seal hunters of my generation putrefy raving die from tuberculosis" (p. 59) to the igloo haiku of

O plump and delicious one
here in land of so short night
me
alone,
humble,
hungering

(p. 69)

At the same time, having noted that the demand in metropolitan Canada and beyond for hand-carved Eskimo sculpture exceeds the supply, Atuk has set up a basement factory run by relatives brought down from Baffin Bay, whom he keeps in line by dispensing the bounty of television, Playboy calendars, and other tawdry cultural items. But Atuk's urban rise is not untroubled.

An Eskimo elder — his arguments drolly reminiscent of a Jewish patriarch warning against the dangers of intimacy with the goyim — urges Atuk to return to the Baffin Bay fold; the relatives working in the basement factory become fractious, and eventually the death of Mush-Mush has to be arranged. The penultimate blow is the discovery of the remains of an American officer on duty in the Arctic and of proof that Atuk had eaten him.

The Incomparable Atuk is nicely paced, and laced with comic invention; and its quick cuts are supplemented by a traditional feature of comic fiction: a social gathering in which most of the characters are brought together. Towards the end of this short novel, however, Richler's inventiveness begins to flag, the brisk to give way to the bizarre: an RCMP officer, *en travesti*, wins the Miss Canada pageant; and Atuk, persuaded to appear on Twentyman's all-Canadian quiz program *Stick Out Your Neck*, is guillotined on camera for failing to answer a question concerning one of the few staples of Canadian common culture — hockey. Though it is perhaps unfair to so unpretentious a fiction, one might even say that in its closing section *The Incomparable Atuk*, like all sendups of topical subjects, runs the risk of becoming an epitome of the schlock it spoofs.

While it is important to understand what kinds of novels Richler has written, recognition of their generic differences is not more critically important than recognition of their thematic and presentational similarities. Take, for example, the "naturalistic" *A Choice of Enemies* (1957) and *Cocksure* (1968), a "straight satire." Norman Price and Mortimer Griffin, the central characters of each novel, both live in London and are professionally connected with the city's artistic and creative worlds. Both are Canadian WASPs of good family; both have in the past acquitted themselves with distinction on the battlefield, a heroism associated with the traditional conservative values of their upbringing. In the present, however, such values have come to seem vestigial, what the earlier novel calls "the fossil[s] of a sillier age, like the player-piano."[52] Both Norman and Mortimer have come to espouse enlightened liberal values and to move in like-minded left-wing circles. In *A Choice of Enemies*, the circle is the *émigré*

North American political liberals who were in Spain and consorted with communism during the 1930s but find themselves increasingly at bay during the reactionary 1950s; in *Cocksure*, it is the swinging liberals of the 1960s, with their flaunted sexual liberation and radical chic.

Unlike the other members of their circles, Norman and Mortimer are liberals of the best traditional sort: undoctrinaire, hypersensitive of conscience, self-questioning. In each novel, events come to undermine the foundations of each character's enlightened values, a destabilization influenced in each case by Jewish shadow figures: Karp in *A Choice of Enemies*, Shalinsky in *Cocksure*. As the sands shift under them, Norman and Mortimer both become at odds with their liberal friends, whose communal beliefs are shown to have become solidified into a new orthodoxy, conformist rather than open-minded, intolerant rather than humane. As a result of the clash between individual and group, both become increasingly isolated, ineffectual, and value-less; and both finally come to a bad end.

A Choice of Enemies is an intelligent, inventive, and rather undervalued novel, on the whole a stronger and more engaging, though a much less professionally polished, performance than *Cocksure*. Of course, the technical and stylistic crudities irritate (Richler was still only in his mid-twenties when the novel was published). The point of view jumps around unnecessarily, especially in the opening chapters; the prose calls rather too much attention to itself; there are some too explicit passages of thematic summary (though it is fair to say that this is a weakness Richler has never chosen to overcome). And there are more serious flaws: the two clinkers in the plot, Norman's amnesia and Ernst's murder of Norman's brother (the latter inessential to plot or theme in the first place and necessitating a one-chance-in-a-million coincidence); and the badly fudged confrontation scene between Norman and Ernst, the former Hitler Youth. But these infelicities are more than compensated for by the strengths of the novel: the group portrait of the blacklisted writers, directors, and producers; the subtlety and depth of the characterization of Norman Price (he is, for instance, shown to have a non-*émigré* feel for London life that is an index of his superior sensibility, just as other incidents are indicative of his finer conscience); and other strong characterizations that help to dramatize the complexities of liberal humanism and the search for necessarily nonabsolute values.

But what finally remains most vividly in the memory concerning *A Choice of Enemies* is its dark negating vision, which ultimately leaves shattered the novel's humane and moral concerns. It is, of course, possible to read *A Choice of Enemies* in such a way as to discern the constructive moral seriousness and the positive conclusion that are for some critics the hallmarks of an artistically successful fiction and the substance of their critical discourse. Take, for example, Bruce Stovel's introduction to the New Canadian Library edition of the novel. Stovel finds at the end of *A Choice of Enemies* a positive conclusion to Norman Price's "apprenticeship": he "fights his way back to an honest self-scrutiny, to a separate peace, to a determination to struggle for success in his marriage and his work."[53] But what I find is a worn out, morally numbed man passively sinking into a marital limbo with a shallow, opportunistic, and ugly wife; in the novel's final sentences, Norman's mind plays host to an utterly banal thought while he pours himself a stiffer drink.

This demoralizing conclusion is hardly unprepared for; in the stories of three other characters, the black hole into which Norman falls is prefigured. There is Charlie Lawson, the Canadian hack writer, a self-pitying loser and emotional slob. He and his long-suffering wife are given an uplifting reconciliation scene, but it is so maudlin and soap-operish ("We could make a fresh start"; "...how vulnerable we both are"; "Help me to live" [pp. 195–96]) as to be cloying rather than cleansing—a hack scene for a hack writer. Distaste hardens into revulsion when near the end of the novel, having made it in Toronto as he never could in London, Charlie is seen on a Canadian television screen mouthing nationalist platitudes about "our gifted poets" (p. 240). There is Sally, the high-minded North American innocent who has come to London seeking romance and adventure but ends up a kept woman spending her days with phenobarbital, gin, double features, and sleeping pills. She dies from an overdose of the last at the same time that her absent sugar daddy, a dissimulator, an adulterer, and a liberal, who hopes to talk her into an abortion, gets sloppily drunk while thickly insisting, "...I'm a humanist....I believe that human life is sacred. That was and still is my position" (p. 235). And finally there is Karp, the concentration-camp survivor, who with his grotesque appearance, wrenching memories, repugnant habits, and psychotic disposition — "The best ones were killed, Karp," Norman shouts at him, "only the conniving, evil ones like you survived" (p. 173) — stands, like Bernanos' Monsieur Ouine, as a powerful image of an obscene spiritual void beyond the reach of humane or moral concerns.

This deconstructive power is also present in *Cocksure*, and it has not gone unremarked by Leslie Fiedler, who describes the novel as "a book which seems always on the verge of becoming truly obscene, but stops short, alas, at the merely funny."[54] The black-humour strain in *Cocksure* is principally found in one of the novel's two narrative lines: that involving Richler's most fantastic invention, the Star Maker, the malign demiurge of the film industry who aspires to divine status through self-reproduction, is destroying humane literary values, and who — in the high point of the novel's dark exuberance — recalls how Hollywood entrepreneurs of the 1930s, "a handful of kikes, dagos, and greaseballs" (p. 162), came to perfect the manufacture of handsome WASP robots called Goy-Boys, mechanical images of desire for the masses.

But as Fiedler intimates, this strain does not infect all of *Cocksure*, which in its other narrative line is, in the main, content to be not blackly comic or absurdist but wickedly funny about a number of excesses of the programmatically emancipated liberals of the 1960s. There is Beatrice Webb House, the school attended by Mortimer's young son: a work by the Marquis de Sade is chosen for its Christmas play; slang terms for the male member are elicited in class; and at parent-teacher meetings there are arguments over whether it is backsliding to forbid masturbation in certain rooms and outside prescribed hours or whether classes of twelve-year-old girls ought to be streamed into those who do and those who don't. There is Mortimer's wife, Joyce, who is "absolutely in touch, thoroughly with it" (p. 33). She calls her husband "a cesspool of received WASP ideas" (p. 23); tells her horrified son it is "Balls" to deny that he secretly desires to make physical love to her in order to supplant his father; terrorizes the greengrocer with her concern for the ideological purity of the fruit; and stops shaving her armpits when she begins an affair with Mortimer's best friend — the hirsute writer and film director Ziggy Spicehandler, né Gerald Spencer, who has rejected his upper-middle-class background and expensive education for the licence of the counter culture, including the opportunity to proclaim on camera that "...so long as you couldn't pull your cock on TV his artistic freedom was impaired" (p. 69).

But while *Cocksure* is not, on the one hand, a black farce (though it has elements of such, which at times approach the obscene), it is not, on the other hand, a satire because it does not imply a standard of values against which deviations and perversions can be measured. Indeed, one of the few ways in which the Canadianness of *Cocksure* might be pointed up is to note that, while the American Leslie Fiedler was complaining that its obscenity was intermittent, the English critics Philip Toynbee and John Wain were complaining about the work's unsatisfactoriness as satire: the former could not "detect the moral platform on which Mr. Richler is standing and from which his darts are launched";[55] the latter noted that Richler "lashes out without having a definite place to lash out *from* — all these modern absurdities are ridiculed, but in the name of what?"[56]

In its failure to be either fish or fowl, *Cocksure* ultimately disappoints as a serious work of fiction. The principal reason why the part of the novel castigating contemporary mores does not solidify into a satire is the inconsistent treatment of Mortimer Griffin, the central character. Mortimer is alternately a target of the satire and, as both naïf and reliquary of traditional values, the lens by which the objects of satire are focused. The gap between Mortimer's "mounting anxieties about the size of his thingee" (p. 105) and his penile chart, on the one hand, and his moral probity and Victoria Cross, on the other, is enormous, and no attempt is made to bridge it.

The reasons why the "obscene" tendencies of *Cocksure* keep collapsing back into the "merely funny" are less apparent, but I can offer one hypothesis. It has to do with Richler's growing fixation with gamy sexuality (it is even more pronounced in *St. Urbain's Horseman* and *Joshua Then and Now*). This fixation is insufficiently assimilated into the texture and themes of *Cocksure*, and its instances remain rather gross adhesions to the text. George Woodcock relates these features "to the world of sexual fantasy and bawdy jokes that beguiles adolescent boys" and lets the matter go at that.[57] But the fact that part of Richler's imagination seems arrested at the level of the high-school lavatory wall is an important matter. One is not arguing that his imagination is tainted by preoccupations he should have outgrown and that he should clean up his act. One's complaint is exactly the opposite: that Richler has been too genteel to allow the lewd and the gross fully to possess his imaginative processes, come what may. To do so might lead to a discomforting shifting of the sands for a writer habituated to satirical and moral themes; but it might also be salutary. Not only might it lead to the transformation of these themes into the truly obscene; it might also have an ultimately positive effect on one of his most serious weaknesses as a writer of realistic fiction: his self-confessed inability (as pronounced as Hemingway's) to create convincing female characters.

All of *Cocksure* was written in one of the interstices in the composition of *St. Urbain's Horseman* (1971), the long-gestating novel that should have been what several reviewers claimed it was: Richler's major achievement. The novel gives evidence everywhere of technical maturity and full stylistic control, and combines the subjects, themes, and modes of the earlier novels in ways that suggest — as does the high seriousness of its epigraph — that Richler was attempting a cumulative fictional statement of his views on the mores and values of contemporary man. But while *St. Urbain's Horseman* is a solid success on the level of superior fictional entertainment, on the level of serious fiction it must be reckoned a disappointment. It doesn't deliver the goods and does not merit either the praise or the detailed exegesis it has been given by a number of critics.[58]

The centre of the novel is a crisis point in the life of Jake Hersh, a successful thirty-seven-year-old "alienated Jew," "modishly ugly," with a gorgeous wife and three children.[59] A Canadian living in London and connected with the city's artistic worlds, of liberal convictions and sensitive conscience, Jake is clearly meant to be the definitive portrait, this time Jewish, of the Norman Price / Mortimer Griffin figure. There are two generic components of Jake's crisis: the advent of the mid-life crunch (Samuel Johnson is cited in this regard), which is triggered by a sense of professional unfulfilment and intimations of mortality; and the cumulative malaise of Jake's "American generation" — "Always the wrong age. Ever observers, never participants. The whirlwind elsewhere" (p. 87) — with its attendant feelings of guilt (Jake even feels a "burden of responsibility" over enjoying a

"singularly happy marriage" [p. 298]). Both these components
are called attention to throughout the novel and are rather too
neatly summarized in the long last chapter of its third part.
(Another component of Jake's crisis, the quandaries of a Canadian artist of his generation, is developed only briefly and drops
from sight about a third of the way through the book.)

In his crisis, Jake fails to navigate successfully between the
Scylla and Charybdis of his voyage into middle age. One rock is
Harry Stein, a striking variation on the Karp / Shalinsky figure.
Repellent in appearance and manner, both of which bespeak
"inherited discontent exacerbated by experience," "black,
wintry experience" (p. 63), Stein is a product of the East London
slums who has become a minor criminal and major injustice
collector. He sees in Jake, who is in worldly terms everything
Stein is not and will never be, an excellent outlet for his
ressentiment. While he can call Stein an "obscene little autodi-
dact" (p. 360), Jake is clearly fascinated by him and even feels a
"sneaking admiration" (p. 340). The other rock is Jake's older
cousin Joey, a mysterious figure who seems in reality nothing
more than a migrant criminal with a certain panache, perhaps
even the moral equal of Harry Stein. But Jake recreates Joey in
the image of his need as an heroic figure who perhaps had been in
Madrid in 1938 and with Trotsky in Mexico soon after and who
in the present time is imagined to be in Paraguay on the trail of
Dr. Mengele. In Jake's recurrent dream, Joey is "Out there,
riding even now. St. Urbain's Horseman. Galloping, thundering.
Look sharp, Mengele, *Die Juden kommen!*" (p. 377). Uncle Abe
may observe that if Joey does find Mengele "... he won't kill him,
he'll blackmail him" (p. 411), and it is later reported by the Canadian consul in Asunción that at the time of his death in an air
crash he had been engaged in smuggling cigarettes; but even at
the end of the novel, Joey remains for Jake a graven image of
possibility, without which he cannot live.

The thematic skeleton of *St. Urbain's Horseman* is, then, solid
and substantial; it is in its incarnation that the weakness of the
novel lies. Everything depends on the presentation of Jake, especially of his mental life and the deeper reaches of his character,
and on the intensity of the reader's sympathetic involvement with
him. Unfortunately Jake is characterized rather too superficially.
One is told, for example, but never shown, that he is charged

with contradictions concerning his professional life; and, for all the time devoted to what is going on in his head, he does not really seem to have much mental life. Despite the big issues Jake is said to be struggling with, *St. Urbain's Horseman* can hardly claim serious attention as a novel of ideas. There are a number of interesting similarities of theme, presentation, and subject matter between Richler's novel and Saul Bellow's splendid novel of ideas, *Herzog*, which Richler in a 1965 *Spectator* review called "a major work of fiction," "a brilliant revelation of character... filled with incident and marvellous inventions, zany characters,... memorable dialogue," and "sensually exact" detail.[60] But comparison of the two re-creations of the mid-life crisis of a representative contemporary man can only cause Richler's novel to shrink into relative insignificance.

Another serious shortcoming is that Jake is treated with too much indulgence. I do not mean to say that he is idealized. It is, of course, true that he is shown to be drolly neurotic, irrationally insecure, resentful, and ignoble; and he is not spared the demeaning affliction of a cherry-sized haemorrhoid. But, on the whole, Richler seems to have assumed that Jake's sensitivities, difficulties, needs, and muddled liberal values are so inherently appealing and widely shared that only a few broad strokes—slipping a secret-agent message into his son's notebook, obsession with the Holocaust, loyally employing down-and-outers for his film crews, reacting as he does to Mouth and Foot Society paintings shown him by Mrs. Ormsby-Fletcher—will suffice to secure the reader's sympathetic involvement. Richler does indirectly try to supply Jake with a dark underside, but he is unsuccessful in giving the reader a convincing sense of the twisted self within. When, at the end of the anticlimactic Old Bailey trial (shades of Leon Uris' *QB VII*), the judge asks, "How in God's name could you form an association with Stein in the first place?" (p. 450), Jakes makes no reply, but the reader is meant to know the answer: that Harry Stein is Jake's *Doppelgänger*, the objectification of his darker self, and that this secret affinity, as much as Jake's guilt feelings over his worldly success, is the bond between them. But the reader can make this connection merely cerebrally. The Harry Stein within Jake remains unknown and unfelt.

Another point is that while Jake's story is the single narrative line in *St. Urbain's Horseman*, it in fact takes up only about half the novel's pages. The rest of the material, related only tangentially to his *crise*, is crisply deployed and excellent as entertainment, but its very abundance tends ultimately to work against the novel's serious aspirations. The best known of the novel's self-contained bits (they were, in fact, separately published as short stories) have English settings: the dinner with Ormsby-Fletcher and the Sunday softball game on Hampstead Heath. But most of the sketches and episodes relate to Jake's Jewish Montreal background: the scenes involving his mother, Herky, Hanna, and Jenny, and the splendid sad / funny chapter describing the Hersh family's week-long mourning for Issy, Jake's father. It is true that the seed of Jake's fascination with the Horseman was sown in his Saint Urbain Street adolescence when, seeking to shape an identity for himself in opposition to his stifling family world, he first becomes Joey's advocate. Since, however, the subject of *St. Urbain's Horseman* is the quandaries of a Jew who has made it out of the ghetto and into the larger world, and not the story of a Jew who is trying to make it, the re-creation of the Saint Urbain world, the particular time and place that Richler has elected himself to get right, does not become an integral part of the novel and does little to intensify its exploration of mores and morals.

But since the Montreal scenes, especially *shivah* for Issy Hersh, involve the author's personal past and touch his root of piety, they do contribute something to the emotional and intellectual *apport* of the novel's conclusion, which has the same quality of Jewishness that has been observed in other novels. Just as the Scylla and Charybdis of Jake's mid-life crisis are Jewish, so is his haven. After hearing of the Horseman's death, Jake is moved deeply and even experiences a liberating moment of emotional release:

> He wept. . . . The tears he couldn't coax out of himself at his father's graveside or summon up for Mr. Justice Beal's verdict on Harry or his mother's departure flowed freely now. Torn from his soul, the tears welled in his throat and ran down his cheeks. He whimpered, he moaned. He sank, trembling, to the sofa. He wept for his father, his penis curling out of his underwear like a spent worm. His penis, my maker. Rotting in an oversize pinewood casket. He

wept for his mother, who deserved a more loving son. He wept for Harry, fulminating in his cell and assuredly planning vengeance. He wept for Nancy, whose stomach was seamed from childbearing. Who would no longer make love with the lights on. He wept because the Horseman, his conscience, his mentor, was no more. (p. 464)

And when, in the novel's last paragraph, Jake takes out the Horseman's journal, crosses out what he had earlier written — "died...in an air crash" — and writes "presumed dead" in its place (p. 467), the reader recalls the words of the wise Jew Chaim at the end of *The Acrobats*: "There is always hope. Always. There has to be."

In 1972, the year after the publication of *St. Urbain's Horseman*, Richler made the difficult decision to leave London, where he had lived for almost two decades, and return to his native Montreal: "...what really impelled me, after years of vacillating, to finally pack my bags was a recurring fear of running dry....looking around, counting heads, survivors, it suddenly seemed to me that too many other expatriate commonwealth writers, writers I respected, had been driven in exile to forging fictions set in the past, the usually dreaded future or, indeed, nowhere."[61] *Joshua Then and Now* (1980), the first fictional fruit of Richler's return, is set in post-November 1976 Quebec (Montreal and the Eastern Townships). But the difference in venue is unimportant compared with the essential similarity between it and *St. Urbain's Horseman*. The sad truth is that Richler's return to his native city did not stimulate his creative powers and lead to an extension of range or deepening of vision. *Joshua Then and Now* was a considerable disappointment, indeed a major blow, to those who had hoped Richler had the dedication to become a superior contemporary novelist.

Jake Hersh and Joshua Shapiro are both coeval with their creator. They are given quasi-creative occupations — Joshua is a sports columnist, television personality, and author of several books. Both drink a lot, have lovely gentile wives, and happy family lives. Both are tough, sardonic, and drolly neurotic on the outside, good-hearted and humane within. In present time, both have reached a crisis point in middle age, the precipitates of which are gradually disclosed. Their generic difficulty was identified by Richler as early as 1956 when he spoke to Nathan Cohen of the difficulty of finding "values with which in this time a man can live with honour." Both novels are equipped with pretentious epigraphs from well-known poems of W. H. Auden, through which Richler vicariously attempts to suggest the high seriousness of both characters' *crise*. Jake and Joshua are baffled liberal humanists ("... I can tolerate everything about the left but its advocates" [p. 250], says the latter), and both regret they were too young to have taken part in the last unequivocally good cause — the Spanish civil war. And like their creator, both have an *idée fixe* about Germans and Jews. Jake's obsession with Dr. Mengele in the jungles of Paraguay has its parallel in Joshua's obsessive memory of Dr. Mueller, the ex-Nazi whom he had encountered during a stay on Ibiza in the early 1950s.

The presentational method of *Joshua Then and Now* is as much a repetition of *St. Urbain's Horseman* as is the central character. In both novels, incidents in the crunch time of the present are repeatedly made to trigger memories which set in motion several story lines, from one to another of which Richler adroitly cuts, deftly juggling then and now. This method has several advantages. It allows the author to bring on stage at intervals one-dimensional characters of whom the reader would soon have his fill if their appearances were prolonged. It also facilitates interpolation of the incidental vignettes, skits, anecdotes, and aperçus that give both novels much of their crackle. In addition, the interweaving of various story lines and the canny withholding of information stimulate the reader's interest in seeing how the various pieces of the central characters' lives will fit together. At the same time, they give the illusion of depth, implicitly suggesting that some significant pattern is emerging. But this presentational method also has its disadvantages, and the reader of *Joshua Then and Now* comes to feel that Richler has made things too easy for himself, that he has not faced up to the problems of structure, theme, and characterization presented by a long novel, but has settled for getting as much mileage as possible out of his material. Fireworks look spectacular in the immediate darkness, but morning reveals a mess of wire and cardboard.

While they last, however, the pyrotechnics are a delight, and on the level of superior fictional entertainment there is much to recommend *Joshua Then and Now*. There are, for example, the wry observations on contemporary English-speaking Montreal, where almost everybody Joshua knew was "inclined to stumble out of bed at 3 a.m. to jot down a list of redeemable assets on the back of an envelope. Or study French verbs" (p. 65). There are a variety of comic characters from Montreal's Jewish world: Joshua's father, Reuben, ex-prize fighter and minor racketeer; Uncle Oscar and his crackpot schemes for making a fortune; and Jake's old classmates from Fletcher's Field High School, including Yossel Kugelman, who has become the esteemed psychiatrist, Dr. Jonathan Cole, author of *My Kind, Your Kind, Mankind*; Irving Pinsky "once celebrated for the sneakers he let rip in Room 42, FFHS" (p. 127), now a rich dentist, "resplendent in a burgundy velvet dinner jacket," serving twenty-five-year-old cognac in "birdbath-size snifters" (p. 127); Izzy Singer the financier, who is unsuccessful at buying his way into the Senate and has to settle for the Order of Canada; and Seymour Kaplan, who takes to wearing black satin panties with a delicate lace trim as a way of curbing his compulsive promiscuity. In addition there are a number of funny set pieces: for example, Joshua's bar-mitzvah, at which his mother does a striptease; the meetings of the William Lyon Mackenzie King Memorial Society, at which Joshua and his Saint Urbain Street contemporaries annually meet to dishonour the memory of the mean-spirited prime minister of their boyhood; and the scene in which Molly Kaplan, scourge of the Jewish General Hospital, mistakenly forces her schmaltzy acceptance-of-death therapy on an elderly furrier in hospital to have his prostate removed.

But however successful as entertainment, *Joshua Then and Now* does not make the grade as serious fiction. As with *St. Urbain's Horseman*, the major problem is the superficial characterization of the central character. Richler apparently feels that Joshua Shapiro (like Jake Hersh) is so inherently engaging that the reader's sympathetic participation in his story can be taken virtually for granted; and that his *crise* is so *à la mode* that a few signposts are sufficient to indicate depth of character. In *The Apprenticeship of Duddy Kravitz*, Aunt Ida remarks, "The human personality is like an iceberg. Nine-tenths of it remains submerged."[62] But almost all of Joshua's personality is above the waterline. The depiction of his political consciousness goes little beyond the reader being told early on that a Republican poster from the Spanish civil war is "his most cherished possession" (p. 5). Later one is told that on a visit to England during the 1960s Joshua was "all at once... filled with a fierce resentment against style-making London, the new modish foolery" (p. 279), but the nature and the intensity of the resentment are not shown, let alone explained. Elsewhere the author simply quotes from Maimonides' *Guide for the Perplexed* ("a book Joshua had come to cherish" [p. 189]) when he wants to strike a philosophical note about good and evil. (Exactly the same passage from Maimonides had been used by Richler as the epigraph for the second part of *The Acrobats*. The reason for this recycling would seem to be authorial sloth.) And lest one be in any doubt about his ethical stature *vis-à-vis* the WASPs of Westmount and Lake Memphremagog, Richler has Joshua's wife, Pauline, spell matters out: "You turned out to be more moral than we were. Possibly because you're new to it" (p. 409). In the key relationship between Joshua and Pauline, the weakness of the former's characterization is compounded by Richler's difficulty in creating convincingly rounded female characters. Their past happiness is merely asserted, as is the intensity of Pauline's love for her ne'er-do-well brother, whose suicide triggers her off-stage breakdown and the temporary disappearance that is ended by her unexplained reappearance, which enables *Joshua Then and Now* to conclude with a soft-centred, unearned tableau of marital felicity among the growing vegetables.

In short, whatever might be incidentally asserted about Joshua's thoughts and feelings, the reader is never shown that he has an inner life, let alone that he is deeply troubled. His consciousness and his crisis, his past and present, are only nominally the centre of a novel which is essentially a collection of professionally presented types, incidents, and observations. One recalls John Fowles's comments about those postwar American novelists who have such "skill at describing, at cutting, at dialogue, at all the machinery; and then at the end one takes the sunglasses off and something's gone wrong. One hasn't a tan."[63]

The Richler novel that gives the deepest tan is *The Apprenticeship of Duddy Kravitz*, the story of a Jewish boy making it out of the Montreal ghetto and the author's most sustained attempt to make a case for an unsympathetic character. But however memorable, the novel is hardly a masterwork. Published when

35

Richler was only twenty-eight, *Duddy Kravitz* is rough-hewn in style, technique, and characterization. It is excellent that Richler's natural voice as a novelist, which is brisk and predominantly comic, has replaced the portentousness and artificiality of that of his first three novels; but the tone is in places uncertain, and the control of pace imperfect. The reader's response to the central character is sometimes mechanically manipulated, and some of the other characters are thinly and unconvincingly rendered, particularly Yvette, the leading female player, a *québécoise* who speaks English as if her mother tongue were Yiddish rather than French. Indeed, it is hard not to think it unfortunate that the novel did not present itself to Richler at a later stage of his career, when his talents and skills had matured and he was fully in control of them. Had this been the case, the story of Duddy Kravitz' apprenticeship in life might have been able to withstand comparison with, say, V.S. Naipaul's *A House for Mr. Biswas*; as it stands, however, the novel is different only in degree from works like Schulberg's *What Makes Sammy Run?*, a similarity called attention to within the text when one character notices Duddy's presence at a reception: "'Well,' he said, 'look who's here. Sammy Glick'" (p. 147).

At first glance, *The Apprenticeship of Duddy Kravitz* looks like a naturalistic novel which dispassionately studies the determining influence of environment on character. Come what may, Duddy has determined in adolescence not to be a loser like his father: "If you want to bet on something then bet on me. I'm going to be a somebody and that's for sure" (p. 94). Duddy's father, a cab driver and part-time pimp, his values and beliefs defined by Eddy's Cigar and Soda, is (after Duddy) the finest characterization in the novel. Max Kravitz is a reprise of Wolf Adler, the father in *Son of a Smaller Hero*. His staleness of mind and vacuity of spirit are mainly registered through his speech, which is laced with banal generalizations: "Anatomy's the big killer..." (p. 106) sums up his knowledge of medical school; and his opinions on weight lifting also encapsulate his views on the social contract: "A guy's got to keep in shape, you know. This world is full of shits. When you meet one and he gives you a shove you want to be strong enough to shove him back. Right?" (p. 172).

The Kravitz family also includes the grandfather, Simcha,

towards whom Duddy feels an exceptional (for him) tenderness and piety. It is his *zeyda* who gives Duddy his first piece of worldly advice: "A man without land is nobody" (p. 49). After graduation from Fletcher's Field (the novel's first sixty pages describe incidents from his high-school years) and a summer as a waiter in a Laurentian resort hotel (the subject of the next forty pages), Duddy's apprenticeship begins in earnest: "You've got to start operating, he told himself. It's getting late" (p. 113). In the outside world, Duddy comes into contact with various exemplars of success or failure: Peter John Friar, director of documentary films and dipsomaniac, whose expertise Duddy needs to realize his idea of making films of weddings and bar-mitzvahs; Jerry Dingleman, the Boy Wonder, whose praises Max continually sings; Hugh Thomas Calder, the Westmount millionaire who takes an interest in Duddy; and Mr. Cohen, the self-made man who gives Duddy advice at a crucial moment: "There's not one successful businessman I know, Duddy, who hasn't got something locked in the closet.... A plague on all the *goyim*.... So a *goy* is crippled and you think you're to blame. Given the chance he would have crippled you.... They're all Nazis. You scrape down deep enough and you'll see" (pp. 266–68).

As his story progresses, Duddy's crudity, abrasiveness, and unscrupulousness are abundantly illustrated; even his Uncle Benjy tells him, "...you're a *pusherke*. A little Jew-boy on the make. Guys like you make me sick and ashamed" (p. 244). Particularly distasteful is Duddy's callous treatment of the devoted Yvette, who is in love with him. But the reader nevertheless continues to feel some sympathy for Duddy, and Richler is careful to keep his central character's rise in a complex perspective. His older brother Lennie, for example, is correct in observing, "You have no code of honour, Duddy. That's your trouble" (p. 186). But Lennie is himself in deep trouble because he has been persuaded to perform an abortion by his "swell bunch" of honourable-seeming gentile friends, who do not really care for him. Mr. Calder may be offended when Duddy introduces a business proposition into their friendship, but the deal is made all the same. And while Uncle Benjy regards his nephew as a *pusherke*, he has no clear answer when Duddy asks, "You think I should be running after something else besides money? Good. Tell me what" (p. 244).

It is the ambivalent response to its central character that brings into focus the moral concerns of *The Apprenticeship of Duddy Kravitz*. For while the feel of the novel is naturalistic, the reader soon realizes that the story of Duddy's apprenticeship is overlaid by a moral pattern. The novel's opening section, told largely from the point of view of Mr. MacPherson, details Duddy's harassment of his ineffectual teacher, which culminates in Mrs. MacPherson's death and her husband's going irreversibly to pieces. Duddy is clearly responsible for the MacPhersons' tragedy, but one does tend to judge him lightly: he is only a teenager, after all, and could not have foreseen the grim results of his actions. During the course of the novel, Duddy is given the opportunity to accept responsibility for what he has done and, through Yvette's love and Virgil's friendship, to grow into a responsible, other-regarding person and to cultivate nonacquisitive values. But Duddy can rise only to the moral level of Becky Sharp in *Vanity Fair* (who thought she could be a good woman if she had five thousand a year): "All I needed was to be born rich. All I needed was money in the crib and I would have grown up such a fine, lovable guy. A kidder. A regular prince among men. God damn it to hell, he thought, why was I born the son of a dope?" (p.302).

The major crisis of Duddy's apprenticeship is precipitated by a serious accident to Virgil, the kindly epileptic who is as loyal to Duddy as is Yvette. Duddy is clearly responsible for what has happened, and in his subsequent broodings, which bring to a stop his frantic business activities, he comes to ponder the death of Mr. MacPherson's wife as well as Virgil's injuries. But he also ponders Cohen's dog-eat-dog advice, and when a newspaper headline suggests to Duddy a fresh source of capital, his *pusherke* side again comes to the fore. In the concluding section of the novel, Duddy cruelly betrays Yvette and Virgil. His grandfather refuses to have anything to do with the land Duddy has acquired; this condemnation of his conduct reinforces the reader's and makes it clear that while his apprenticeship has culminated in material success (and finally won him Max's approval), it has also ended in human and moral failure.

Much of the critical comment on *Duddy Kravitz* praises the novel for its mixture of slice-of-life realism (an authentically observed time and place) and serious moral concern. But I would urge that the novel's moral pattern is rather too schematic and clear-cut, is hardly a challenging fictional subject — it is that of hundreds of North American novels and films — and is, in fact, one of the weaker features of a novel that might well have been a stronger performance had it been more thoroughly naturalistic in technique and eschewed the moral overlay. Had it been so, the major source of the strength of *Duddy Kravitz* would have been more readily identifiable: the raw drive of the title character, who is Richler's most forceful and memorable creation at least partly because he is an incarnation of the dark, negating energy of Richler's imagination. Duddy may be placed in a moral context, but the frame is ill-adapted to the picture. Duddy is a grating amoral force who is all undirected drive and aggression. His needs are deep and compulsive, but because he does not know what they are he does not know how to satisfy them. For most of the novel, the object of his desire is possession of the secret lake and its environs — in one scene, his gaze remains fixed on them even while making love with Yvette. At moments, however, Duddy seems obscurely to sense that the source of his deepest needs lies elsewhere and is connected with his father and mother. But his father is emotionally empty, a defensive failure, a pimp and a dope, with nothing to give; and his mother is long dead. Duddy's deepest needs will never be satisfied no matter how hard he runs, though they do become more and more covered by the garish scab of material success. It is this demoralizing psychological datum, much more than his imputed moral failure, that stunts and ultimately withers Duddy's humanity even as it fuels his destructive personality, and that makes him (when he reappears in *St. Urbain's Horseman*) speak deeper than he knows when he exclaims, "Who in the hell could love Duddy Kravitz?" (p. 211).

In this critical overview of Richler's fiction, a contrast between his early novels and his later ones has been noted. While the first four — *The Acrobats* through to *The Apprenticeship of Duddy Kravitz* — were technically crude and (with the exception of the last) heavily serious, they did have energy, passion, and a raw sincerity rooted in a dark vision of human possibility. The four later novels — *The Incomparable Atuk*, *Cocksure*, *St. Urbain's Horseman*, and *Joshua Then and Now* — were much more technically proficient, but either had less energy and passion or had these qualities less consistently present. There was still rawness, but it tended to be found in a gratuitous grossness that could remind one of Irving Howe's comment on Philip Roth: that his is "a creative vision deeply marred by vulgarity."[64] If one had a prediction to make, it would be that in the years before him Richler will continue to offer superior fictional entertainments informed by moral concern and leavened with satiric bite, but that unless his gamy fixations are transformed and the rough beast at the nadir of his vision can once again shoulder its way into the pages of his fiction, he will probably not be able to offer more. On the other hand, there can be no doubt that in the years behind him — a writing career of over thirty years — Mordecai Richler has produced some of the best, and certainly the most widely entertaining, Canadian fiction of his generation.

NOTES

[1] Louis Rosenberg, *Canada's Jews: A Social and Economic Study of the Jews in Canada* (Montreal: Bureau of Social and Economic Research, Canadian Jewish Congress, 1939), p. 31.

[2] Mordecai Richler, *The Street* (Toronto: McClelland and Stewart, 1969), p. 10.

[3] Nathan Cohen, "A Conversation with Mordecai Richler," *The Tamarack Review*, No. 2 (Winter 1957), pp. 6–23; rpt. in G. David Sheps, ed., *Mordecai Richler*, Critical Views on Canadian Writers, No. 6 (Toronto: McGraw-Hill Ryerson, 1971), p. 24. All further references to this work (Cohen) appear in the text.

[4] "The Expatriate Who Has Never Left Home," *Time* [Canadian ed.], 31 May 1971, pp. 8–9.

[5] See Mordecai Richler, "A Sense of the Ridiculous: Notes on Paris 1951 and After," in *Shovelling Trouble* (Toronto: McClelland and Stewart, 1972), pp. 23–46.

[6] Mordecai Richler, "How I Became an Unknown with My First Novel," *Maclean's*, 1 Feb. 1958, p. 40.

[7] For a full listing of Richler's periodical writings, see Michael Darling, "Mordecai Richler: An Annotated Bibliography," in *The Annotated Bibliography of Canada's Major Authors*, ed. Robert Lecker and Jack David, 1 (Downsview, Ont.: ECW, 1979), 161–78. All further references to this work (Darling) appear in the text.

[8] For information on the Richler-Kotcheff friendship, and on the filming of *The Apprenticeship of Duddy Kravitz*, see Martin Knelman, "You See, Duddy, You See?" in *This Is Where We Came In: The Career and Character of Canadian Film* (Toronto: McClelland and Stewart, 1977), pp. 99–114.

[9] "O Canada," in *Hunting Tigers under Glass: Essays and Reports* (Toronto: McClelland and Stewart, 1968), p. 15.

[10] Robert Fulford, Introd., *The Great Comic Book Heroes and Other Essays*, New Canadian Library, No. 152 (Toronto: McClelland and Stewart, 1978), p. 7.

[11] Mordecai Richler, "The Elected Squares (2): Foreigners in Etobicoke," *Spectator*, 24 March 1961, p. 393.

[12] Mordecai Richler, "The Elected Squares (3): The White Americans," *Spectator*, 7 April 1961, p. 469.

[13] "The Elected Squares (3): The White Americans," p. 469.

[14] John Metcalf, "New Novels," rev. of *A Flame for Doubting Thomas*, by Richard Llewellyn, *The Acrobats*, by Mordecai Richler, and *African Diversions*, by Ernst Juenger, *Spectator*, 23 April 1954, p. 503.

[15] *The Acrobats* (London: André Deutsch, 1954), p. 48. All further references to this work appear in the text.

[16] *Cocksure* (Toronto: McClelland and Stewart, 1968), pp. 229, 230. All further references to this work appear in the text.

[17] John Metcalf, "Black Humour: An Interview with Mordecai Richler," *Journal of Canadian Fiction*, 3, No. 1 (Winter 1974), 73, 74. All further references to this work (Metcalf) appear in the text.

[18] George Woodcock, "Richler, Mordecai," in *Contemporary Novelists*, 2nd ed., ed. James Vinson (London: St. James, 1976), p. 1169.

[19] "Letters in Canada 1954: Fiction," *University of Toronto Quarterly*, 24 (April 1955), 262.

[20] "Letters in Canada 1955: Fiction," *University of Toronto Quarterly*, 25 (April 1956), 306.

[21] Robert Weaver, "Canadian Fiction," rev. of *Son of a Smaller Hero*, and five other books, *Queen's Quarterly*, 63 (Spring 1956), 129.

[22] Nathan Cohen, "Heroes of the Richler View," *The Tamarack Review*, No. 6 (Winter 1958), pp. 47–60; rpt. in Sheps, ed., *Mordecai Richler*, p. 57.

[23] Naïm Kattan, "Mordecai Richler: Craftsman or Artist," *Canadian Literature*, No. 21 (Summer 1964), pp. 46–51; rpt. in Sheps, ed., *Mordecai Richler*, pp. 92–98.

[24] Warren Tallman, "Politics Neglected," rev. of *Son of a Smaller Hero* [New Canadian Library ed.], *Canadian Literature*, No. 30 (Autumn 1966), pp. 77–79; rpt. in "Four Takes on Mordecai Richler's Fiction," *Open Letter*, 3rd ser., No. 6 (Winter 1976–77), pp. 50–52. See also Donald Cameron, "Don Mordecai and the Hardhats," *The Canadian Forum*, March 1972, pp. 29–33; and Robin Mathews, "Messiah or Judas: Mordecai Richler Comes Home," *Canadian Review*, 1, No. 1 (Feb. 1974), 3–5.

[25] Leslie Fiedler, "Some Notes on the Jewish Novel in English," *The Running Man*, 1, No. 2 (July–Aug. 1968), 18–21; rpt. in Sheps, ed., *Mordecai Richler*, pp. 99–105.

[26] Roger Sale, "What Went Wrong?" rev. of *The Blood Oranges*, by John Hawkes, *The Tenants*, by Bernard Malamud, *St. Urbain's Horseman*, by Mordecai Richler, and *Wonderland*, by Joyce Carol Oates, *The New York Review of Books*, 21 Oct. 1971, p. 4.

[27] "Horsing Around," rev. of *St. Urbain's Horseman*, *The Times Literary Supplement*, 3 Sept. 1971, p. 1045.

[28] George Woodcock, "The Wheel of Exile," rev. of *St. Urbain's Horseman*, *The Tamarack Review*, No. 58 (1971), pp. 65–72.

[29] Ofelia Cohn-Sfetcu, "Of Self, Temporal Cubism, and Metaphor: Mordecai Richler's *St. Urbain's Horseman*," *International Fiction Review*, 3, No. 1 (Jan. 1976), 30–34.

[30] Wilfred Cude, "The Golem as Metaphor for Art: The Monster Takes Meaning in *St. Urbain's Horseman*," *Journal of Canadian Studies*, 12, No. 2 (Spring 1977), 50–69.

[31] *Canadian Literature*, No. 29 (Summer 1966), pp. 7–17; rpt. in Sheps, ed., *Mordecai Richler*, pp. 1–14.

[32] Bruce Stovel, Introd., *A Choice of Enemies*, New Canadian Library, No. 136 (Toronto: McClelland and Stewart, 1977), pp. vii–xv.

[33] John Moss, *Patterns of Isolation in English-Canadian Fiction* (Toronto: McClelland and Stewart, 1974), pp. 227–30, 235–37.

[34] Margot Northey, "Satiric Grotesque: *Cocksure*," in *The Haunted Wilderness: The Gothic and Grotesque in Canadian Fiction* (Toronto: Univ. of Toronto Press, 1976), pp. 95–100.

[35] John Moss, *Sex and Violence in the Canadian Novel: The Ancestral Present* (Toronto: McClelland and Stewart, 1977), pp. 123–25, 131–39, 144–45.

[36] See above, note 7.

[37] "Why I Write," in *Shovelling Trouble*, p. 19.

[38] *Son of a Smaller Hero* (London: André Deutsch, 1955), p. 9. All further references to this work appear in the text.

[39] A. M. Klein, "Autobiographical," in *The Second Scroll* (New York: Knopf, 1951), p. 126.

[40] George Eliot, "Brother and Sister," in *Complete Poems* (Boston: Dana Estes, n.d.), p. 394.

[41] Graeme Gibson, "Mordecai Richler," in *Eleven Canadian Novelists Interviewed by Graeme Gibson* (Toronto: House of Anansi, 1973), p. 271. All further references to this work (Gibson) appear in the text.

[42] Donald Cameron, "Mordecai Richler: The Reticent Moralist," in *Conversations with Canadian Novelists* (Toronto: Macmillan, 1973), Pt. II, p. 117. All further references to this work (Cameron) appear in the text.

[43] *The Street*, p. 15.

[44] James Wolcott, "Kvetchy but Unbowed," rev. of *Joshua Then and Now, The New York Review of Books*, 17 July 1980, p. 36.

[45] *Joshua Then and Now* (Toronto: McClelland and Stewart, 1980), pp. 315, 314. All further references to this work appear in the text.

[46] Walter Goodman, "Mordecai Richler Then and Now" [interview], *The New York Times Book Review*, 22 June 1980, pp. 11, 22.

[47] A. Alvarez, "Beyond All This Fiddle," in *Beyond All This Fiddle: Essays 1955–1967* (New York: Random House, 1969), pp. 7–8.

[48] Hugo McPherson, "Fiction 1940–1960," in *Literary History of Canada: Canadian Literature in English*, 2nd ed., gen. ed. and introd. Carl F. Klinck (Toronto: Univ. of Toronto Press, 1976), II, 225.

[49] George Eliot, *The Mill on the Floss* (Oxford: Clarendon, 1980), p. 238.

[50] George Woodcock, Introd., *Son of a Smaller Hero*, New Canadian Library, No. 45 (Toronto: McClelland and Stewart, 1965), pp. vii–xii; rpt. in Sheps, ed., *Mordecai Richler*, p. 17.

[51] *The Incomparable Atuk* (Toronto: McClelland and Stewart, 1963), p. 7. All further references to this work appear in the text.

[52] *A Choice of Enemies* (London: André Deutsch, 1957), p. 253. All further references to this work appear in the text.

[53] Stovel, Introd., *A Choice of Enemies*, p. xiv.

[54] Fiedler, p. 105.

[55] Philip Toynbee, rev. of *Cocksure, London Magazine*, May 1968, pp. 77–79; rpt. in Sheps, ed., *Mordecai Richler*, p. 108.

[56] John Wain, "Puppeteers," rev. of *The Three Suitors*, by Richard Jones, *Cocksure*, by Mordecai Richler, *Enderby*, by Anthony Burgess, and *Love and Work*, by Reynolds Price, *The New York Review of Books*, 22 Aug. 1968, p. 34.

[57] George Woodcock, *Mordecai Richler*, Canadian Writers, No. 6 (Toronto: McClelland and Stewart, 1971), p. 50.

[58] See, for example, John Moss, "Richler's Horseman," in *The Canadian Novel: Here and Now*, ed. John Moss (Toronto: NC, 1978), pp. 156–65.

[59] *St. Urbain's Horseman* (Toronto: McClelland and Stewart, 1971), p. 17. All further references to this work appear in the text.

[60] "The Survivor," rev. of *Herzog*, by Saul Bellow, *Spectator*, 29 Jan. 1965, p. 139.

[61] Mordecai Richler, "Going Home Again," *The New York Times Book Review*, 1 Sept. 1974, p. 10.

[62] *The Apprenticeship of Duddy Kravitz* (London: André Deutsch, 1959), p. 239. All further references to this work appear in the text.

[63] John Fowles, "I Write Therefore I Am," *Evergreen Review*, 8, No. 33 (Aug.–Sept. 1964), 17.

[64] Irving Howe, "Philip Roth Reconsidered," in *The Critical Point: On Literature and Culture* (New York: Horizon, 1973), p. 155.

SELECTED BIBLIOGRAPHY

Primary Sources

Books

Richler, Mordecai. *The Acrobats*. London: André Deutsch, 1954.
———. *Son of a Smaller Hero*. London: André Deutsch, 1955.
———. *A Choice of Enemies*. London: André Deutsch, 1957.
———. *The Apprenticeship of Duddy Kravitz*. London: André Deutsch, 1959.
———. *The Incomparable Atuk*. Toronto: McClelland and Stewart, 1963.
———. *Cocksure*. Toronto: McClelland and Stewart, 1968.
———. *Hunting Tigers under Glass: Essays and Reports*. Toronto: McClelland and Stewart, 1968.
———. *The Street*. Toronto: McClelland and Stewart, 1969.
———, ed. *Canadian Writing Today*. Harmondsworth, Eng.: Penguin, 1970.
———. *St. Urbain's Horseman*. Toronto: McClelland and Stewart, 1971.
———. *Shovelling Trouble*. Toronto: McClelland and Stewart, 1972.
———. *Notes on an Endangered Species and Others*. New York: Alfred A. Knopf, 1974.
———. *Jacob Two-Two Meets the Hooded Fang*. Toronto: McClelland and Stewart, 1975.
———. *Images of Spain*. Photographs by Peter Christopher. Toronto: McClelland and Stewart, 1977.
———. *The Great Comic Book Heroes and Other Essays*. Introd. Robert Fulford. New Canadian Library, No. 152. Toronto: McClelland and Stewart, 1978.
———. *Joshua Then and Now*. Toronto: McClelland and Stewart, 1980.

Contributions to Periodicals

Richler, Mordecai. "How I Became an Unknown with My First Novel." *Maclean's*, 1 Feb. 1958, pp. 18–19, 40–42.

———. "The Elected Squares (2): Foreigners in Etobicoke." *Spectator*, 24 March 1961, pp. 393–94.

———. "The Elected Squares (3): The White Americans." *Spectator*, 7 April 1961, pp. 468–69.

———. "The Survivor." Rev. of *Herzog*, by Saul Bellow. *Spectator*, 29 Jan. 1965, p. 139.

———. "Going Home Again." *The New York Times Book Review*, 1 Sept. 1974, pp. 10–12.

Secondary Sources

Bissell, Claude. Rev. of *The Acrobats*. In "Letters in Canada 1954: Fiction." *University of Toronto Quarterly*, 24 (April 1955), 262.

———. Rev. of *Son of a Smaller Hero*. In "Letters in Canada 1955: Fiction." *University of Toronto Quarterly*, 25 (April 1956), 305–07.

Bowering, George. "And the Sun Goes Down: Richler's First Novel." *Canadian Literature*, No. 29 (Summer 1966), pp. 7–17. Rpt. in *Mordecai Richler*. Ed. G. David Sheps. Critical Views on Canadian Writers, No. 6. Toronto: McGraw-Hill Ryerson, 1971, pp. 1–14.

Cameron, Donald. "Don Mordecai and the Hardhats." *The Canadian Forum*, March 1972, pp. 29–33.

———. "Mordecai Richler: The Reticent Moralist." In *Conversations with Canadian Novelists*. Toronto: Macmillan, 1973. Pt. II, pp. 114–27.

Cohen, Nathan. "A Conversation with Mordecai Richler." *The Tamarack Review*, No. 2 (Winter 1957), pp. 6–23. Rpt. in *Mordecai Richler*. Ed. G. David Sheps. Critical Views on Canadian Writers, No. 6. Toronto: McGraw-Hill Ryerson, 1971, pp. 22–42.

———. "Heroes of the Richler View." *The Tamarack Review*, No. 6 (Winter 1958), pp. 47–60. Rpt. in *Mordecai Richler*. Ed. G. David Sheps. Critical Views on Canadian Writers, No. 6. Toronto: McGraw-Hill Ryerson, 1971, pp. 43–57.

Cohn-Sfetcu, Ofelia. "Of Self, Temporal Cubism, and Metaphor: Mordecai Richler's *St. Urbain's Horseman.*" *International Fiction Review*, 3, No. 1 (Jan. 1976), 30–34.

Cude, Wilfred. "The Golem as Metaphor for Art: The Monster Takes Meaning in *St. Urbain's Horseman.*" *Journal of Canadian Studies*, 12, No. 2 (Spring 1977), 50–69.

Darling, Michael. "Mordecai Richler: An Annotated Bibliography." In *The Annotated Bibliography of Canada's Major Authors.* Ed. Robert Lecker and Jack David. Vol. 1. Downsview, Ont.: ECW, 1979, 155–211.

"The Expatriate Who Has Never Left Home." *Time* [Canadian ed.], 31 May 1971, pp. 7–11.

Fiedler, Leslie. "Some Notes on the Jewish Novel in English." *The Running Man*, 1, No. 2 (July–Aug. 1968), 18–21. Rpt. in *Mordecai Richler.* Ed. G. David Sheps. Critical Views on Canadian Writers, No. 6. Toronto: McGraw-Hill Ryerson, 1971, pp. 99–105.

Fulford, Robert, introd. *The Great Comic Book Heroes and Other Essays.* New Canadian Library, No. 152. Toronto: McClelland and Stewart, 1978, pp. 7–10.

Gibson, Graeme. "Mordecai Richler." In *Eleven Canadian Novelists Interviewed by Graeme Gibson.* Toronto: House of Anansi, 1973, pp. 265–99.

Goodman, Walter. "Mordecai Richler Then and Now" [interview]. *The New York Times Book Review*, 22 June 1980, pp. 11, 22–24.

"Horsing Around." Rev. of *St. Urbain's Horseman. The Times Literary Supplement*, 3 Sept. 1971, p. 1045.

Kattan, Naïm. "Mordecai Richler: Craftsman or Artist." *Canadian Literature*, No. 21 (Summer 1964), pp. 46–51. Rpt. in *Mordecai Richler.* Ed. G. David Sheps. Critical Views on Canadian Writers, No. 6. Toronto: McGraw-Hill Ryerson, 1971, pp. 92–98.

Knelman, Martin. "You See, Duddy, You See?" In *This Is Where We Came In: The Career and Character of Canadian Film.* Toronto: McClelland and Stewart, 1977, pp. 99–114.

Mathews, Robin. "Messiah or Judas: Mordecai Richler Comes Home." *Canadian Review*, 1, No. 1 (Feb. 1974), 3–5.

McPherson, Hugo. "Fiction 1940–1960." In *Literary History of Canada: Canadian Literature in English.* 2nd ed. Gen. ed. and introd. Carl F. Klinck. Toronto: Univ. of Toronto Press, 1976. II, 205–33.

Metcalf, John. "New Novels." Rev. of *A Flame for Doubting Thomas*, by Richard Llewellyn, *The Acrobats*, by Mordecai Richler, and *African Diversions*, by Ernst Juenger. *Spectator*, 23 April 1954, p. 503.

———. "Black Humour: An Interview with Mordecai Richler." *Journal of Canadian Fiction*, 3, No. 1 (Winter 1974), 73–76.

Moss, John. *Patterns of Isolation in English-Canadian Fiction.* Toronto: McClelland and Stewart, 1974, pp. 227–30, 235–37.

———. *Sex and Violence in the Canadian Novel: The Ancestral Present.* Toronto: McClelland and Stewart, 1977, pp. 123–25, 131–39, 144–45.

———. "Richler's Horseman." In *The Canadian Novel: Here and Now.* Ed. John Moss. Toronto: NC, 1978, pp. 156–65.

Northey, Margot. "Satiric Grotesque: *Cocksure.*" In *The Haunted Wilderness: The Gothic and Grotesque in Canadian Fiction.* Toronto: Univ. of Toronto Press, 1976, pp. 95–100.

Sale, Roger. "What Went Wrong?" Rev. of *The Blood Oranges*, by John Hawkes, *The Tenants*, by Bernard Malamud, *St. Urbain's Horseman*, by Mordecai Richler, and *Wonderland*, by Joyce Carol Oates. *The New York Review of Books*, 21 Oct. 1971, pp. 3–4, 6.

Stovel, Bruce, introd. *A Choice of Enemies.* By Mordecai Richler. New Canadian Library, No. 136. Toronto: McClelland and Stewart, 1977, pp. vii–xv.

Tallman, Warren. "Politics Neglected." Rev. of *Son of a Smaller Hero* [New Canadian Library ed.]. *Canadian Literature*, No. 30 (Autumn 1966), pp. 77–79. Rpt. in "Four Takes on Mordecai Richler's Fiction." *Open Letter*, 3rd ser., No. 6 (Winter 1976–77), pp. 50–52.

Toynbee, Philip. Rev. of *Cocksure. London Magazine*, May 1968, pp. 77–79. Rpt. in *Mordecai Richler.* Ed. G. David Sheps. Critical Views on Canadian Writers, No. 6. Toronto: McGraw-Hill Ryerson, 1971, pp. 106–09.

Wain, John. "Puppeteers." Rev. of *The Three Suitors*, by Richard Jones, *Cocksure*, by Mordecai Richler, *Enderby*, by Anthony Burgess, and *Love and Work*, by Reynolds Price. *The New York Review of Books*, 22 Aug. 1968, pp. 34–35.

Weaver, Robert. "Canadian Fiction." Rev. of *Son of a Smaller Hero*, and five other books. *Queen's Quarterly*, 63 (Spring 1956), 126–30.

Wolcott, James. "Kvetchy but Unbowed." Rev. of *Joshua Then and Now. The New York Review of Books*, 17 July 1980, pp. 35–36.

Woodcock, George, introd. *Son of a Smaller Hero.* By Mordecai Richler. New Canadian Library, No. 45. Toronto: McClelland and Stewart, 1965, pp. vii–xii. Rpt. in *Mordecai Richler.* Ed. G. David Sheps. Critical Views on Canadian Writers, No. 6. Toronto: McGraw-Hill Ryerson, 1971, pp. 15–21.

———. *Mordecai Richler*. Canadian Writers, No. 6. Toronto: McClelland and Stewart, 1971.

———. "The Wheel of Exile." Rev. of *St. Urbain's Horseman*. *The Tamarack Review*, No. 58 (1971), pp. 65–72.

———. "Richler, Mordecai." In *Contemporary Novelists*. 2nd ed. Ed. James Vinson. London: St. James, 1976, pp. 1165–69.